TEAM MEMBER'S MANUAL

VACATIONS WITH A PURPOSE

A Handbook for Your
Short-Term Missions Experience

CHRIS EATON AND KIM HURST

Cook Ministry Resources
a division of Cook Communications Ministries
Colorado Springs, Colorado/Paris, Ontario

SINGLE MINISTRY RESOURCES is a division of Cook Communications Ministries. In fulfilling its mission to encourage the acceptance of Jesus Christ as personal Savior and to contribute to the teaching and putting into practice of His two great commandments, Cook Communications Ministries creates and disseminates Christian communication materials and services to people throughout the world. SINGLES MINISTRY RESOURCES provides training seminars, a national convention, a journal, and resource materials to assist churches in developing a ministry with single adults that will encourage growth in loving God and each other.

Vacations With a Purpose
Team Member's Manual

Cook Ministry Resources
a division of Cook Communications Ministries
4050 Lee Vance View, Colorado Springs, CO 80918-7100

The song "I Love You, Lord" on page 70 is reprinted with the permission of Maranatha! Music, Laguna Hills, California.

Thanks to those who contributed: Adele Calhoun, Jean Stephens, and Steve Webb.

Cover photography: Mike Marshall

Printed in the United States of America.

ISBN: 0-7814-5041-1

CONTENTS

To Carey Caldwell and Rich Hurst,

*who have played such significant roles in our lives,
our ministries, and our understanding of the process
and importance of short-term mission teams.*

AUTHORS

Chris Eaton is president of Bridge Builders, Inc., a consulting group that assists churches in developing short-term mission teams and programs. Formerly, he was the executive director of Single Purpose Ministries, a decade-old, interdenominational singles ministry in Florida.

During his tenure with Single Purpose, Chris began developing curriculum to assist short-term teams. Over the past eight years he has facilitated numerous teams involving several hundred adults. He is also a frequent speaker at singles groups around the United States.

Kim Hurst is one of the founders and former coordinators of the Vacations with a Purpose program at the University Presbyterian Church in Seattle, Washington, a 3,500-member church.

The curriculum and program policies developed at University Presbyterian Church have been used successfully by many churches wanting to implement short-term mission teams.

Kim's interest in other cultures was stimulated by a period of travel as a member of Up With People. She has led or trained numerous short-term mission teams to more than a dozen countries. Kim is the former Director of Missions at the Crystal Cathedral in California and did graduate work at Fuller Seminary. Kim and her husband, Rich, have two daughters and live in Colorado.

ACKNOWLEDGMENTS

This book, and the teams it describes, could not have existed without the prayers and hard work of many concerned people who helped us at every stage. We'd like to express our thanks to those who have contributed so much to the short-term mission programs at Single Purpose Ministries and University Presbyterian Church and to those who have encouraged and assisted us with this book. We are both indebted to Carey Caldwell and Rich Hurst who were partners with us at every step. Many of the ideas in this book (especially in chapters 9, 10, and 14) originated with them.

There were also many others who contributed to the experiences that we drew upon to write this book. At the risk of omitting some, we'd like to especially mention Jerry O'Leary, Bruce Larson, Art Beals, John Westfall, Rob Turner, Rob Phillips, Nancy Nielsen, Traci Anderson, Jeff Hussey, Jim Vasquez, Linda Menke Vasquez, Sandy Gwinn, Laurie Krinke, Karen Fledderman, Jim Towry, Wanda Grewe, and the Board of Directors of Single Purpose Ministries, Inc.

We'd also like to thank those who read and commented on the manuscript (even though we didn't heed all of your advice, we sincerely appreciate it): Adele Calhoun, Park Street Church in Boston; Henry Williams, Westlink Christian Church in Wichita; Carey Caldwell, Bridge Builders, Inc., in St. Petersburg; Jerry O'Leary, University Presbyterian Church in Seattle; and Doug Millham, Discover the World, Inc., in Pasadena. Also, our thanks go to Jerry Jones for seeing the importance of this project and for giving us the much-needed encouragement to keep going and to meet our deadlines.

Finally, we wish to thank the scores of team leaders, team members, missionaries, and hosts whose lives have been interwoven through Vacations with a Purpose, and who provided the inspiration for this book.

NAME PAGE

Vancouver 1st Church of God

TEAM

Vicki Scheel

NAME

3112 SE Silversprings DR

ADDRESS

Vancouver WA 98683

CITY, STATE, ZIP

(360) 254-8183

PHONE NUMBER

Randy Scheel

NAME OF CLOSEST RELATIVE

( ) Same

PHONE NUMBER OF CLOSEST RELATIVE

Husband

RELATIONSHIP

PASSPORT NUMBER

EMERGENCY NUMBER ON FIELD

Pacificare

INSURANCE CARRIER

INSURANCE NUMBER

PROJECT

PART ONE
GETTING STARTED

CHAPTER ONE

WHAT IS A VACATION WITH A PURPOSE?

Welcome to Vacations with a Purpose, an exciting experience. Your decision to become involved in this adventure can be one you will treasure for years. There are few other ways to learn as much about yourself, another culture, other people, or your relationship with God. You will see, experience, feel, and learn more than you can imagine. And all in such a short period of time!

In order to make this the best possible experience, you have work to do prior to your departure date. This book is designed to enhance your experience. But it will only do that if you use the contents as your team leader(s) directs. For your VWAP (Vacation with a Purpose) to be all it can be, proper preparation is essential. Having watched several hundred people go on these trips, we can assure you that without exception those who took the time to prepare greatly enhanced their experience and growth.

THIS IS YOUR BOOK

At the conclusion of the trip this book will contain a rather complete history of your experiences. We encourage you to write in this book during trip preparation, on site, and after you are home. Several years from now, when the memories have faded, you will be able to look at this book and be challenged by the things you went through, the things you learned, and the people you met.

Our hope is that your VWAP will change your life. May this book assist in that endeavor.

VACATIONS WITH A PURPOSE

What comes to mind when you hear the term? You may react like most hardworking adults: Every vacation has a purpose—to get away from the job and take it easy. Some crave peace and quiet, while others cannot wait to escape the humdrum of everyday living and embark on an adventure. They long to meet new and interesting people, travel to faraway places, feast on exotic dishes, and collect stories to take back to the office.

This book is for those who are ready to step beyond normal routines and quiet vacations into the exciting world of short-term missions. Vacations with a Purpose, or VWAPs (pronounced Vee-Waps), are short mission trips that give people the opportunity to meet new friends, live in community, experience a different culture, and best of all, see God at work.

The phenomenal growth of short-term mission teams, or VWAPs, reflects our ever-shrinking world and our ever-growing appetite for intercultural exposure. Doug Millham, the founder of the church mobilization program called Discover the World, whose doctoral dissertation dealt with short-term missions, states that between 1979 and 1989 the numbers of people involved per year in short-term missions rose from just over 25,000 to approximately 120,000. Concurrently, the number of agencies involved with short-termers has grown from fifty to more than 400! Churches and parachurch organizations offering such programs are besieged by requests by church leadership seeking information and assistance in developing programs of their own.

Mission agencies are also noticing that career-aged professionals (who can't imagine living abroad for even a few years) thrill at the opportunity to experience cross-cultural missions for their annual vacation. John Huffman, director of Latin American Missions' "Christ For the Cities" program (CFC), has gone so far as to say that "commuter missionaries" are the wave of the future. His organization has been greatly aided and encouraged by teams of properly prepared, energetic team members who have traveled to CFC projects to serve, learn, and form relationships with their Latin brothers and sisters in Christ.

But the list of those who benefit through short-term mission teams extends beyond career missionaries and team participants. Local church pastors are discovering that their entire congregations are affected as well. The men, women, and youth who participate in such an experience begin to develop a greater maturity and become more effective church members. They, in turn, strengthen the whole church. Like many other ideas whose "time has come," the concept of fostering Christian discipleship among congregations through this type of cross-cultural involvement is one that many are realizing simultaneously.

An example of how this idea occurred to several people at once is found in our own stories. We didn't know each other in the early 1980s when we each had a part in "inventing" the short-term teams program for our ministry groups, yet the programs we helped develop were almost identical.

KIM'S STORY

Vacations with a Purpose began for me in 1985 at University Presbyterian Church in Seattle. Two members of the UPC singles department commented on the beauty of their recent vacations to Mexico. But they felt frustrated that they had been unable to appreciate and know Mexico's finest asset—its people. Was there a way to get to know the people in a short vacation? What if UPC singles could spend their vacation with Mexican Christians? Six of us began to meet and pray about where we might begin.

Within months, the first UPC Vacations with a Purpose team was working in Mexico, hand in hand with missionaries and Mexicans. We intended to "better the lives" of orphaned and abandoned children as well as to aid the poor Indian migrant workers living close by. But as we offered our *hands* to the people we had gone to serve, we discovered something very profound occurring in our *hearts*. The smiles on the children's faces, the words of praise for God on the lips of the poorest field-workers, and the selflessness of the orphanage houseparents were all reaching out and changing us. We went to serve and returned to Seattle profoundly served.

Keeping in mind the word *vacation* in our title, we designed the schedule to conclude with a few days of rest and reflection

17

at the beach in Ensenada. After the physically and emotionally draining days at the project site, we needed time for rest and perspective. Ensenada provided a psychological layover between the mission site and Seattle. Discussions at the meals and evening group meetings centered on making sure that our time in Mexico was not an isolated event. Would we let the experience change us? Would our personal philosophies and identities be marked forever by our venture into missions?

Since that first trip to Mexico, Vacations with a Purpose has expanded to include other countries thus providing adults, both single and married, the opportunity to learn about God through the lives of Christians in many corners of the world. Team members have returned renewed, enlightened, and enthusiastic for ministry. Some have changed careers in midstream and become long-term missionaries. Others have become involved in church leadership as elders and teachers, or have participated in local ministries. Vacations with a Purpose is now one of the church's primary discipleship training tools and involves 300 adults from all sectors of the church. Members of the congregation who have never taken a Vacation with a Purpose have found their own outlook reshaped and their world enlarged through the experiences of former team members.

Our experiences, along with those of people in other churches, have taught us a great deal about what makes a team work. But more importantly, we have learned that there is no limit to the way God can reveal Himself to those who are willing to see Him through the eyes of another.

CHRIS'S STORY

Ironically, my venture into VWAP began with a "failure." In 1983 several lay leaders in Single Purpose, a ministry for single adults in South Florida, expressed interest in "doing something" overseas, something that would fit into their vacation schedules. A trip lasting more than two weeks was out of the question, but a one-to-two-week trip was quite feasible.

A trip was scheduled to Haiti in conjunction with another agency. Planning, recruiting, and training all went smoothly.

But then, one week before the team's departure, work plans in Haiti fell apart. I was left to decide whether or not to go through with the trip. I desperately wanted people to have the opportunity for this type of experience, but I did not want to waste the money that had been invested. In the end, I decided not to take the team to Haiti. But I resolved to take a team the following year and to be more purposeful in the planning.

In 1984 the first Single Purpose short-term mission team went to a school for the deaf outside Port-au-Prince, Haiti. That team began what has become our greatest tool for developing leadership, for discipling our members, and for launching people into ministry and mission. The feedback from host churches and mission agencies with which we have worked has been overwhelming.

Since that first trip, Single Purpose has taken more than 300 people (the majority of whom were single) overseas as part of over twenty-five short-term projects. The teams, composed largely of unskilled laborers, have generally participated in work projects, ranging from building benches to constructing school buildings. All have worked in partnership with the nationals from the particular countries. This sort of cooperation encourages meaningful interaction with the nationals and eliminates the perception that this is merely a "North American" project.

VWAP teams often construct buildings, but more importantly, the experience builds lives. After six years, I am still amazed to see how life-changing a one-or-two-week experience can be. As people work, worship, and live with others of a different culture, they learn much about the other culture, and a great deal more about themselves.

When we met in 1987, we discovered our mutual enthusiasm for the benefits of short-term mission teams. We enjoyed comparing notes about travel hints, proper training, spiritual applications, and so on. We also found that numerous churches were eager for information on starting teams. Furthermore, former team members wanted better training before they went, as well as better tools to help them process the experience once home.

The result of those conversations is this book.

VWAP DEFINED

Just what is a Vacation with a Purpose? How is it different from any other vacation? What distinguishes it from any number of Christian tour groups? Let's start with a definition.

A Vacation with a Purpose is a short-term trip involving a group of people seeking the opportunity as a team to:

- experience a different culture,
- interact personally with individuals of that culture,
- serve the nationals and/or Christian workers in the culture, and
- become "world Christians" through personal and spiritual growth derived from the experience.

The statement above provides a good working definition for Vacations with a Purpose, but let's make certain we share the same terminology.

Short-Term

For the purposes of this book short-term means one to two weeks in length. (We write this at the risk of offending those who have given their entire lives to missionary service and consider anything less than five years "short-term," and anything less than two years, unthinkable!) Today, travel is such that a team can arrive at a destination in only one day, whereas in the past the trip may have taken several weeks! Thus, shorter trips with a considerable amount of time in the host community are more feasible.

Team

A Vacation with a Purpose is more than a group of individuals who spend time traveling on the same bus and eating at the same restaurants. Team building, team growth, and teamwork are integral components of the experience.

Experience a Different Culture

Due to increased media coverage, people today are able to catch glimpses of and experience secondhand various cultures around the world. A secondhand experience is not as compelling as a hands-on interaction with a culture, however. So a great many of today's adults are seizing opportunities to personally encounter the people of the cultures they have seen.

A different culture is not necessarily a non-North American one. Some cultures throughout the United States and Canada may be worlds apart from your own: inner-city poor, native Americans, and ethnic groups are a few examples.

Interact Personally
To have meaningful opportunities to work alongside members of the host community, worshiping, working, and living together.

To Serve
To make a significant and encouraging contribution, *as defined by the host group.*

World Christians
Followers of Jesus Christ with an increasing awareness of their membership in, and responsibility to, the global community. These are people whose commitment to the spiritual, physical, and emotional health of their world neighbors stems from their own relationship with Jesus Christ.

CHAPTER TWO

WHY GO ON A VACATION WITH A PURPOSE?

66 Jill took a deep breath of the salty sea air and soaked in the sights of the dusty mission station where she had just arrived with her twenty teammates. A young orphan's tiny hand in hers felt somehow comforting and familiar in this strange place. Over the laughter of children, she heard the groans of the passing school buses on their way to disgorge tired field-workers in the tin and cardboard shantytown that was their home. After months of work as part of the VWAP (Vacations with a Purpose) leadership team, Jill was finally seeing the orphanage and meeting the people she had been praying for. Like the others on her team, Jill had practiced her Spanish, prepared songs, games, and lessons for the vacation Bible school, and prepared her heart to help the missionaries in whatever way she could.

As the days passed, the long hours she spent clearing rocks and brush where a church foundation would be poured seemed fulfilling, not as tedious as she imagined. She was somehow uplifted by the hard work, especially when she and her teammates would sing old spirituals, much to the delight of the nationals working with them.

But it was the evenings that meant the most to her. After a hard day of labor, she enjoyed the chance to gather with her team and talk about the day. During those talks, everything she had been seeing and feeling seemed to come together. She thought about the few hours of gracious hospitality shown by the shantytown family she had visited, how they had offered her an upended crate for a stool and a few berries spirited home from the fields as a meal. She listened as a team member cried in confusion and sadness that so many godly people were living in such squalor, while the food they were harvesting was destined for the tables of those who had never known hunger.

Jill nodded in agreement as another teammate shared how he had been touched by the Sunday service. Everyone, it seemed, had been there: his coworkers, the immaculately groomed town doctor, the dirty and sickly village children and their weary parents, and the missionaries. Each one with arms and voices raised in praise to the God of them all.

For a few days after returning home, she enjoyed recounting tales of her two-week Vacation with a Purpose. But with each passing day her little stories rang hollow to her, when she realized that her listeners couldn't really understand the meaning behind them. Then she noticed that the comforts and familiar sights and sounds at home seemed less comforting, less familiar. No longer content to amble by the homeless man who begged for coins near her apartment, she now wanted to know his name, to listen to his story, his hopes, his pains. Racial slurs and jokes about "lazy foreigners" had always made her feel uncomfortable; now they made her angry.

A short time later, Jill realized that she could no longer be content in her cozy, familiar world. She resolved to be an agent of compassion and of change. In whatever small way she could, she would help others to see people as God sees them: each one with a name, a face, a story; each one created in the image of God and for whom Christ had died on the cross.**"**

What happens in the lives of the team members who participate in Vacations with a Purpose? What is the value of investing precious time and money in such short-term ventures? Isn't it better to just send the money spent on a trip to the particular mission site so they can use it as they choose? Wouldn't that be a wiser and more practical use of funds? These are the types of questions you may be asked as you prepare for your trip.

Such questions do not recognize the potential impact a trip can make on you, your team members, your colleagues, and your church. Like Jill, you too can be challenged, changed, and redirected by your Vacation with a Purpose. The needs in the world become less and less like "Sixty Minutes," something you can watch and turn off.

Pastor and author Bruce Larson has said that when God wants to teach us something He takes us on a trip. Travel seems to be one of God's favorite primers for teaching us about Himself. In confronting the unfamiliar we learn to see things as they really are. Remember how John Bunyan's pilgrim learned about the truth in his journey away from the comforts of home? Or recall how the patriarch Joseph was plucked as a boy from his family and sent on a journey to Egypt where he learned about God's miraculous providence. In Mark Twain's classic *The Prince and the Pauper* Prince Edward learned many of life's important lessons during his days as a commoner. God has specific things to teach each person on a VWAP trip. But one thing is certain: God wants to teach all of us the mind and character of Jesus Christ (Philippians 2:5). VWAPs exist to make us more like Jesus.

The best way to explain why someone should go on a VWAP is to mention the benefits to you, your local church, and the nationals in the host country.

BENEFITS TO YOU

Experience That Will Stretch You
As you experience a different culture, people, and lifestyle you will find your own life experience is stretched. The whole idea of doing something that requires moving out of your "safe zone" is an experience that will affect you forever.

Exposure That Will Change You
On a VWAP you will be exposed firsthand to needs in a different country/culture. Rarely can one be personally exposed to the starkness of human need and remain unchanged. Coming face to face with authentic needs is to expose yourself to risks and responsibilities that can radically change you!

Education That Will Enlighten You
Reading or hearing about needs in the world can be, and often is, frustrating because you feel powerless to make any significant difference. VWAP participants have the opportunity to

learn issues firsthand (from the people they meet) and discover that they as "short-termers" can make a difference once they are home. In addition, this education process enlightens you to the needs that exist in your day-to-day world. Needs that have always been right in front of your eyes now seem new and noticeable. Your awareness and concern become heightened.

Encounters That Will Affect You
Leaving a familiar environment and placing yourself in a situation where you have to trust in God can lead to powerful experiences. A participant encounters a host of new relationships with members of the host community, team members, missionaries, and supporters. All of these encounters are avenues for encounters with God. Furthermore, one cannot go on a VWAP without encountering oneself. You may not go with this intent, but the whole process may be very revealing.

BENEFITS TO HOST COMMUNITY

What benefits do you and your team offer the members of the church in the host country?

Relational
Members of churches in other countries appreciate the relationships they form with team members. They are excited about the possibilities of developing relationships with North American Christians who will pray for and with them in their work. You will find the souvenir requested most by nationals is your address!

Cultural
You and your team members are not the only ones having a cultural experience. The host group is often amused by the behavior of their visitors, especially the participation of women in traditionally male tasks.

Affirmation
National church members are often renewed and rejuvenated by the simple presence of North Americans who have come to

their area as servants. Your presence, service, and interest all affirm their belief in God's grace and provision.

Financial
Very often God uses the team as a vehicle to answer the prayers of a local congregation. The financial contribution on the field will vary from team to team, but any resources we choose to share can be put to great use (especially in projects in the Third World).

BENEFITS TO YOUR HOME CHURCH

Outward Focus
Often our churches and/or organizations at home can drift into being very inwardly oriented. Energy is focused on only meeting the needs of those who are members or participants. As you and your fellow team members' eyes and hearts are opened to the needs that exist in the world, we hope you will carry that concern home with you. Oftentimes the team's deep concern is a catalyst for stirring up a renewed outward focus for the church. Needs begin to be noticed and addressed in the church's community that were never or rarely noticed before.

Renewal
The personal renewal you experience by participating in a VWAP may well spark renewal in your home church. There is something incredibly contagious about having ten to fifteen people come back into a local church with a renewed desire to seek and serve God. The stretching and challenging you experience may be a means by which God breathes new life into your group at home.

Community
Community is one of those elusive terms that we often hear talked about at our churches but rarely seem to experience. A VWAP challenges you to work, serve, worship, and live with people whom you did not choose. At home we usually choose who we want to be with. Here God has made this choice for us. This team is God's vehicle to train and teach us what it means to pray, to encourage, to work, to listen, and to rely on

one another. Experiencing what Jesus describes as the oneness of the Body of believers can have a tremendous impact on your group at home, if you will continue to pursue community.

PART TWO
GETTING PREPARED

*Think back on the biggest trip you have ever taken.
Wasn't there quite a bit of preparation that went into
it? Chances are, if your answer is no, the trip had its
chaotic moments. Because your leaders want this trip
to be not only a pleasant memory but also an experience that will challenge you for years to come, we have
included a number of "getting prepared" sessions.*

*Now, if you are like us you would probably prefer
to get your bags packed and get down there! That's
why it is important for us to emphasize at this stage
that the Vacation with a Purpose (VWAP) experience
is more than the "on the field" portion of the trip. It
begins with the weeks and months of preparing both
individually and as a team. And it continues with
processing the experience once you are home. While
the "on the field" portion will be the highlight of your
experience, the events leading up to and following from
it sustain and integrate your growth process.*

*The preparation stage can and should be an
enjoyable time of getting to know yourself and your
team members. So we encourage you to think and work
through the material given. By doing so, we believe you
will be allowing God to gradually prepare you for your
Vacation with a Purpose.*

CHAPTER THREE

FINANCING YOUR TRIP

One of the best ways to raise funds for your Vacation with a Purpose is by personally asking people to support you in the experience. Many team members have told us that even though they were initially put off by the idea of sending support letters, it turned into one of the best aspects of the whole adventure. An avid football fan from one team wrote the head coach of his favorite college football team in the Big Ten Conference. His letter explained the purpose of the trip, his hopes and goals, and described the need. The coach, who had never met this young man, sent a check for $250! Another woman sent a letter to the owner of a company that does a lot of business with the firm where she works. Not only did he make a very large donation to the team, but he was very interested in hearing about her experience when she returned.

There are three types of support letters. Discuss fund-raising plans with fellow team members and help them decide which type(s) of letter would be most appropriate.

1. *Letter requesting funds for your trip.*
2. *Letter requesting funds for the project.* Perhaps you have decided to pay for your own trip but wish to ask for donations for the project itself. Explain this, saying that you are asking friends to join in contributing toward the project.
3. *Letter requesting prayer but no money.* Even if you do not need any funds, we encourage you to include others in your VWAP by inviting them to join you in praying for this endeavor.

GUIDELINES FOR FUND-RAISING LETTERS

If you are raising funds for your own participation, consider sending letters to friends, business associates, relatives, and others. The fund-raising letters should include the following:

1. Information about the country/culture you are going to. Include a brief description of the area and things that might be of interest, such as per capita income, literacy rate, population, and so on.
2. Information on the sending organization and the hosting organization. The sending organization is the church or ministry that is planning the trip. The hosting group is the mission agency and/or national church with which you are working.
3. Description of what the team will be doing. Include why the team is doing this particular project. For example, if you are building a rural clinic, why is that a need in the community?
4. The cost of the trip.
5. Why you want to be involved in this trip. Briefly list your reasons for going on the trip. Mention your desire to become more globally aware and develop a deeper faith. But remember, your readers would be more likely to donate money to the support of an actual project or activity they could see you doing.
6. How you would like the reader to be involved. Address why you are asking them to contribute financially. Review the project description mentioned in the third guideline. Ask the reader to assist in supporting this endeavor by contributing to your expenses. This need not be a long "sales pitch," but rather a simple request.
7. Clear instructions on how contributors are to respond, including:

   • Who to make the check payable to (checks should not be made payable to you if the contributor wishes the donation to be tax-deductible).
   • Where to mail it.

- When you need it.
- Whether you are requesting prayer or financial assistance or both.

Make sure you compose your own letter. People prefer to read a personalized letter as opposed to a form letter that is sent by everyone on the team.

Also keep it brief! The first page will probably be read, others may not be.

GROUP FUND-RAISING IDEAS

Several suggestions for raising funds are listed here. You undoubtedly have other ideas of your own. In addition, your public library or church library may have information on the subject. Keep a detailed record of the ideas you use and how successful they are. This record will help in the planning for future teams.

Fun Runs

One large urban church has raised more than $35,000 in scholarships and project costs for the past four years by sponsoring a 10K run/5K walk each spring. The event attracts people of all ages from throughout the church congregation. Funds are raised by runners/walkers who seek sponsors for their participation, and by charging an entry fee to the more serious runners who like running in this officially-timed race. This annual event now has the entire congregation involved in the idea and excitement of Vacations with a Purpose.

Work Days

In another group, participants ask people to sponsor them for their work in some community project. The participant provides eight hours of labor to an organization like Habitat for Humanity or at the home of an elderly or disabled neighbor. Again, in addition to funds raised, the participant has the chance to share his or her enthusiasm for the upcoming trip.

Food Fast

On an individual basis, team members and other supporters can skip one meal a week for a certain number of weeks and give the amount ($5) they would normally spend on the food toward the missions project.

Activities
Plan an event and direct a percentage of the gate receipts toward the project. Design and sell T-shirts or visors promoting the trip. Offer special services around holidays. For example, team members could deliver singing telegrams, balloons, valentines, flowers, or home-made cakes or candies. Contact business owners or social clubs and ask if they will consider donating a percentage from their own fund raisers or public-relations events (e.g., fashion shows, dinners, tennis matches). The Boston Children's Museum donated scores of promotional digital watches to one team going to the Dominican Republic. Due in part to the increased visibility of celebrities working for global concerns, businesses seem willing to contribute to relief efforts.

Auction
A church in New England conducted an auction for their young adult ministry's summer VWAP. People donated their services to be auctioned off: everything from "cleaning out your refrigerator" to "a gourmet meal for four." After two weeks of soliciting services from the group, the auctioning began. This event raised over $3,000 for their team!

IDEAS USED BY THIS TEAM

List your fund-raising ideas here as a record, but be sure to carefully document the specifics elsewhere so you can pass them along to the next team.

FINANCIAL INFORMATION

TEAM COST

_____

DUE DATES FOR MONEY

Date: _____ Amount: _____

Date: _____ Amount: _____

Date: _____ Amount: _____

RECORD OF DONORS

NAME	ADDRESS	AMOUNT
1.		
2.		
3.		
4.		
5.		
6.		
7.		
8.		
9.		
10.		

CHAPTER FOUR

TEAM PREPARATION SESSIONS

As little children we learned about preparation. Our parents prepared us for our first day of school, our first overnight visit and our first week at camp. Boy Scouts learned to "be prepared." And we began races with "One for the money, two for the show, three to get ready, and four to go." But as we grew up we also learned that preparation could be time consuming and difficult. So many of us learned to "wing it." We took shortcuts and hoped for the best. Sometimes things worked out and sometimes disaster struck. In the process we supposedly gained a precious commodity called experience.

Our experience with Vacations with a Purpose (VWAP) leads us to one conclusion: "Do not wing your short-term missions trip." If you are to benefit, grow, and do something constructive for others, you need to prepare. You are not just devoting a portion of your vacation to a short-term mission. You are committing yourself to the time, energy, study, and preparation that are all prerequisites of the trip. If your group is to operate as a unit, as the Body of Christ, then you need time together prior to departure. During team meetings, expectations become clarified, personalities become distinguishable, and skills in group problem solving begin to develop.

The following exercises are designed to aid in team development and preparation. Your team leader will go over the material with you in team meetings. Be sure to familiarize yourself with the content. Completing homework assignments will enable you to benefit from discussions as well as mark your commitment to growth together.

SESSION ONE—AM I READY TO BE A TEAM PLAYER?

Preparation is a key ingredient for a successful and life-changing VWAP. A trip needs leaders. But leaders only begin and facilitate your preparation. The following issues and questions will stimulate your thinking about what it will take to be ready for the trip.

THE TEAMWORK FACTOR

Just what does teamwork mean? What are the traits of a team player? We have come up with fourteen words that form the basis of what we call the "TEAMWORK FACTOR," the traits exhibited by those who are pitching in to do their part for the good of the group.

T is for Teachable
A teachable spirit helps create a noncompetitive environment in which learning and sharing come naturally. Teachability gives all the members the freedom to make mistakes as they learn.

E is for Encouraging
Think of how encouraging words enhance the development of community. What differences do they make?

A is for Appreciative
What things can we appreciate in others on the team? How can we show our appreciation?

M is for Motivated
Take initiative! Do all things as unto the Lord (Colossians 3:17,23).

W is for Willing
Team members may have different levels of strength, skill, and health, but each should be willing to work to the best of his or her capabilities. Willingness also includes accepting uncomfortable conditions in the host country. Willingly take on the heat, food, bugs, and germs.

O is for Open
Be open with what you are learning, experiencing, feeling, thinking, etc. Express both the positive and negative. Your vulnerability with others builds community.

R is for Refreshing
The times may be tough—heat, sickness, exhaustion, physical labor, emotion drain, and so on. In those times it will be incredibly refreshing to have another team member help pick up your spirits! Think about how you can be replenishers to each other on a daily basis.

K is for Kindred Spirit
There's a sense of camaraderie as we pursue this together. We are all part of the Christian family and we're all in this together!

F is for Flexible
Anything can change from day to day. A flexible team member will learn to accept the unexpected as the norm.

A is for Agreeable
Living together in close quarters, sharing crowded bathing facilities, and every other aspect of group travel requires everyone to be gracious.

C is for Cooperative
Share with one another, help and assist one another. Instead of grumbling about problems, propose solutions!

T is for Thoughtful
What can you do to make a teammate's day a little easier?

O is for Obedient
There will be times when the team leader has to "pull rank" and make unpopular decisions. A team player will respect the leader's authority and encourage others to do the same.

R is for Relational
Get to know the others on your team. Go out of your way to learn about their hopes, their dreams, their history.

Get the picture? The "TEAMWORK FACTOR" spells out the difference between a group of isolated individuals and a team of interconnected members.

Now it's your turn to compile your own list of negative traits below, using the first letter shown in each space. Think of words that work against community and destroy team spirit.

N

E

E

M

S

H

E

M

O

D

Now rearrange the letters to find out what you're say-ing to the team when you exhibit these traits.

_____ ___ _____!

PERSONAL PREPARATION

Are You Prepared Physically?

1. Are you in shape? What exercises could you be doing to get in better shape for your particular project (e.g., walking, jog-ging, etc.)?

2. Are you in good health? What steps could you take to improve your health prior to the trip (e.g., diet, sleep, etc.)?

Are You Prepared Emotionally?

3. Are you in shape emotionally? Think through the following questions:

    a. Are there any unresolved issues or relationships in your life?

    b. Are you having any bouts with depression or discouragement that should be talked out prior to your trip?

    c. Would it be wise to talk these out with a pastor, counselor, or friend?

    d. Could you be viewing this trip as some sort of therapy for problems in your life?

    e. If you are, what problems are you trying to "escape" from? Why?

Are You Prepared Spiritually?

4. A mission trip is not the time to be getting things together with God. Instead, you should be developing and improving your relationship with Him now.

a. Reflect on where you are spiritually. What will give you a richer experience if you begin to do it now?

b. *Start listening:* Are you listening to God? Are there quiet times in your day to reflect on what God is teaching you?

c. *Start reading:* Are you spending time reading God's Word? How consistently?

d. *Start speaking:* What's your prayer life like? Are you taking time each day to talk with God?

e. *Start responding:* Are you striving to be obedient in the little things? Are you attempting to apply the things God is teaching you?

Are You Prepared Relationally?

5. You will be spending much of your time with a group of people to whom your experience will be closely tied. Consequently, it is important to think through the way you relate interpersonally.

a. Are you prone to any types of conflict that hinder your ability to work with others? What are they? When are they most likely to occur?

b. Do you consider yourself a good listener? How might this be improved before joining the team?

c. Are you comfortable being transparent with others? What factors determine whether or not you will share with another? What obstacles do you have when it comes to being open and vulnerable?

d. Would you consider yourself to be a cooperative person? Why, or why not? Are there certain circumstances when you find it hard to be cooperative with others? What are they? Do group decisions frustrate you?

Think Through Your Expectations
6. Write down your expectations for this trip in the space below.

7. Go back and make a check by the expectations that could be unrealistic. Why are they unrealistic?

8. How could they be adapted to become more realistic?

9. Have you ever been disappointed due to unrealistic expectations? Explain.

10. As you look over your expectations, what areas of potential disappointment do you see on this trip?

AGREEING TOGETHER—STATEMENT OF POLICIES

Below is a list of policies that you will be asked to commit yourself to while involved in this VWAP. These are not simply rules for rules' sake, but rather policies to help everyone (team members, nationals, mission agency people, etc.) have a positive experience. The first step of working together as a team is agreeing to uphold these items. Your covenant is not so much with the leadership as it is with each other.

Be sure you understand these policies. Feel free to ask your leaders the reasoning behind each of them.

VWAP POLICY STATEMENT

I realize that the following elements are crucial to the effectiveness, quality, and safety of our trip together. As a member of this Vacations with a Purpose team, I agree to:

1. Remember that I am a guest working at the invitation of a local missionary, pastor, medical clinic, etc. If my hosts are offended by bare arms, shirtless backs, or exposed legs, I'll cover them. If they offer me goat meat stew, I'll try it! I'll remember the missionaries' prayer: "Where You lead me, I will follow; what You feed me, I will swallow!"

2. Remember that we have come to learn, not to teach. I may run across procedures that I feel are inefficient, or attitudes that I find closed minded. I'll resist the temptation to inform our hosts about "how we do things." I'll be open to learning other people's methods and ideas.

3. Respect the host's view of Christianity. I recognize that Christianity has many faces throughout the world, and that the purpose of this trip is to witness and experience faith lived out in a new setting.

4. Develop and maintain a servant attitude toward all nationals and my teammates.

5. Respect my team leader(s) and his or her decisions.

6. Refrain from gossip. I may be surprised at how each person will blossom when freed from the concern that others may be passing judgment.

7. Refrain from complaining. I know that travel can present numerous unexpected and undesired circumstances, but the rewards of conquering such circumstances are innumerable. Instead of whining and complaining, I'll be creative and supportive.

8. Respect the work that is going on in the country with the particular church, agency, or person(s) that we are working with. I realize that our team is here for just a short while, but that the missionary and local church are here for the long term. I will respect their knowledge, insights, and instructions.

9. Attend all team preparation classes and follow-up meetings.

10. Fulfill all logistical requirements. I will comply with all requirements regarding passports, finances, shots, and so on.
11. Refrain from negative political comments or hostile discussions concerning our host country's politics.
12. Remember not to be exclusive in my relationships. If my sweetheart or spouse is on the team, we will make every effort to interact with all members of the team, not just one another. If I am attracted to a teammate, I will not attempt to pursue an exclusive relationship until after we return home.
13. Refrain from any activity that could be construed as romantic interest toward a national. I realize certain activities that seem innocuous in my own culture may seem inappropriate in others.
14. Abstain from the consumption of alcoholic beverages or the use of tobacco or illegal drugs while on the trip.

Signed _____ Date _____

Throughout team preparation meetings you will be provided with information about the country or region you will be visiting. You may want to do some additional research on your own. Use the space below to note what you have learned either in your reading or from guest speakers.

① extra glasses
② Toilet Seat cover
③ Powder
④ Don't be stoic. Let someone know if you are not feeling well.
⑤ insect repellant
⑥ pocket knife. pack in suitcase - cant take on plane if over 2"
⑦ wrap bottles etc in baggies
⑧ get small plastic bottles for things
⑨ balance bars
⑩ Rollaboard

MEDICAL PRECAUTIONS

Important: We recommend that you consult your local health department to see which shots and/or medication you need for the area you will visit. Do you need to take precautions against diseases such as typhoid, malaria, and various types of gastric distress? In some cases, there is very minimal reason for concern. On the other hand, many countries require proof of vaccination before you may begin your travel. Be sure you check what applies in the area where you'll be.

In all cases, it is wise to have a current tetanus booster and a supply of Pepto Bismol or similar product for the prevention and/or relief of diarrhea.

Health Guidelines

Duane (Chip) Anderson of Latin American Mission in San Jose, Costa Rica, makes the following suggestions for team members traveling in his area. They seem to make sense for all teams traveling outside of North America.

1. Be sure the water you drink is safe. Drink bottled water or purify tap water before drinking. Avoid ice cubes that are made from tap water; freezing does not kill the offending bacteria.
2. Avoid uncooked vegetables, salads, and fruit that cannot be peeled.
3. Do not eat raw eggs, uncooked meat, or unprocessed cheese.
4. Bring a container of hand towelettes, as washing facilities are not always available.
5. Take your customary medications along with a renewal prescription. Be sure to know the generic names of your prescribed drugs. Also, bring your prescription for eyeglasses. Notify your host and team leader of any special medical needs well before you arrive on the field.
6. When traveling in the tropics, be very careful of the intense sun. Apply sunscreens and wear protective clothing.
7. Pepto Bismol is one of the most effective remedies to prevent and relieve diarrhea. Two tablespoons (or two tablets) is the recommended dosage. If vomiting accompanies diarrhea, refrain from food and drink for one hour, then try a tablespoon of clear liquid every five minutes for one hour.
8. *Notify the team leader and seek professional care* if any of the following occur:

   * diarrhea lasting more than seventy-two hours,
   * bloody diarrhea,
   * persistent or severe abdominal cramps or pain,
   * vomiting lasting more than six to twelve hours,
   * severe chills, and/or
   * painful urination or discharge.

(This material is adapted from "Short-Term Teams Leaders Guide," by Duane Anderson, Christ for the City, LAM, San Jose, Costa Rica, 1989.)

47

Medical Insurance

Long before you leave, check with your private (or Canadian government) carrier to see if you will be covered by insurance while out of the country. If so, find out all the necessary details in case medical care is necessary. For example, will you have to pay out-of-pocket and get reimbursed when you return? What information will the insurance company require you to get while still at the clinic or hospital? Is there a phone number to call if you get hurt?

If you are not covered, check into getting a temporary travelers' policy. These are generally inexpensive. Keep in mind that most missionary agencies require you to have medical coverage.

Medical Requirements for This Team

The particular medical requirements for your team should be noted below. For example, if you are going to use malaria pills, how long before and after the trip do you need to take the dosage? Are you informed of the necessary injections and where they can be obtained? Do they need to be given on a schedule rather than on one day?

1.

2.

3.

4.

5.

6.

As a team member you are "plopped" down in a culture quite a bit different from your own. The behaviors, values, and beliefs of the people may differ greatly from those you are used to. With time you may come to notice the common denominators between yourself and your hosts. But the differences will hit you first.

BEING A BRIDGE BUILDER

Cultural differences might be pictured in the following way. There are two cliffs: On one side is the North American way of life and on the other is the way of life found in the host country. In between looms a large chasm. In order for the two cultures to meet and understand one another a bridge must be built connecting the two sides. Imagine your upcoming journey as an apprenticeship in bridge building. You can lay the beam, erect a scaffolding, and forge cables that make communication between your worlds possible. Surprise your host community with your initiative at bridge building and you will find their hands joining yours.

Building the bridge involves a number of things you can think through before going, as well as others you can work on while you are there. Unfortunately, some people go on short-term teams and never work at building the bridge. They deprive themselves of some very important personal experiences, which tragically limits their understanding and curtails their growth.

Bridge building is an exciting challenge! In fact, we believe you will come to appreciate the world opening to you so much that you will continue to build bridges for the rest of your life.

Bridge Building Involves Examining Your Stereotypes

All of us maintain certain stereotypes about other people. Some are based on elements of truth. Others grow out of myths or false perceptions. It is unfair to judge or evaluate a person based on stereotypes about the group he or she belongs to. God created individuals who are uniquely different, and they should be treated as such.

Building the bridge begins with examining stereotypes: the

ones you may hold and the ones the nationals may hold about you. Let's think through them.

STEREOTYPES NORTH AMERICANS HAVE ABOUT PEOPLE IN THE THIRD WORLD	
NEGATIVE	POSITIVE
Innocent	Interdependent with family
Lazy	Living in harmony with life
Inefficient	Very spiritual
Emotional	Content
Slow	Servant attitude
Indifferent	
Corrupt	
Poor	
Uneducated	
Needing help	
Controlled by customs	

When you arrive in the host country, you will be viewed in a certain way just because you are a North American. Doesn't seem fair, does it? But is there an element of truth in these views? Think about the stereotypes in the following box, then answer the questions in the spaces provided.

STEREOTYPES OTHERS HAVE OF NORTH AMERICANS	
NEGATIVE	POSITIVE
Aggressive	Educated
Harshly pragmatic	Reliable
Tense	Strong individuals
Discontent	Secured better lives
Lonely	Free of superstition
Corrupt	Confident
Wealthy and materialistic	Organized
Dominating	
Loud and obnoxious	
Competitive	
Selfish/self-centered	
Attitude of national superiority	
Preoccupied with efficiency	

Questions for Reflection

1. As you look through this list, what is your reaction? How do you feel?

2. Which of these apply to you? Would others see these in you?

3. Do you feel that you hold some of the stereotypes listed for people in the Third World? Which ones do you think may be valid? Why?

4. How might these stereotypes hinder the bridge-building process?

You cannot change the fact that you are a North American. And you will be perceived stereotypically from time to time. This is not all bad. Stereotypes can have some merit and facilitate understanding. But as you know from experience, not every individual embodies all the characteristics of a particular stereotype. To be a bridge builder you need to understand the reasons behind stereotypes. We bomb the bridge when we judge people without attempting to understand or giving them a chance to explain themselves.

Bridge Building Involves Remembering Your Roles

There are three "roles" you will play that contribute to your ability as a bridge builder.

- *The role of being a "guest" of the culture.* Think of being a guest in someone's home. How would you behave, react, interact, etc.? Or conversely, what expectations would you have of a guest in your home? What might please and/or irritate you?
- *The role of being a "student" of the culture.* Think of yourself as a person who is there to study and learn. How does a student in school get an A? What behaviors contribute to success?
- *The role of being a "servant" within the culture.* Think of being a person who serves everyone he or she encounters in the country. How does a servant approach those whom he or she serves? How does a servant handle differences in others?

Bridge Building Involves the Following Applications

Accepting: Accept the fact that you will not completely understand the people in just one trip. This is just a beginning, so don't become too frustrated with yourself.

Awareness: Be aware that at times you may feel your prejudices. You may become frustrated with the way things are or the way people behave. Don't deny the feelings, own them. Only then can you begin to understand the reasons behind them. Why are you frustrated? Being aware will help you grow in your understanding of differences.

Listening: Listen more than you talk. You are there to learn, not to instruct. The right to instruct is earned by demonstrating respect.

Giving: Give of yourself. Take the initiative in group settings to reach out to the nationals. People can tend to shy away from contact with nationals, especially if they aren't fluent in the language. Go ahead! Take a risk and try to speak the language. People will really appreciate the effort. And don't worry, they'll forgive you when you mess up.

Enjoying: Enjoy the people, their culture, and their language. If you don't take yourself too seriously you can have more fun. Help create an environment where they can enjoy you and your culture and language just as you aim to enjoy theirs.

PERSONAL GOALS

Thoughtfully and prayerfully fill in the following. This will help you think through and crystallize where you want to grow on this trip. It also helps the leader(s) become aware of your personal expectations and potential roadblocks to your goals.

1. The following are three things I hope to learn.

2. The following are three ways I hope to grow.

3. The following are potential roadblocks to my learning and growing.

We continue to build bridges when we include people in our plans and secure prayer support for our venture. Remember that unless the Lord builds the house, they who build it labor in vain.

It's time to scope out all those questions about what you ought to take. So start making your list and checking it twice. If you forget to take something, you may have to live without it for the duration. During this session you may also find out what items you need to carry down for the team project.

PACKING LIST

Personal Items Checklist

- ☐ toothbrush/paste/floss
- ☐ razor/shaving cream
- ☐ sunburn remedies
- ☐ small pillow/sheets/blanket
- ☐ towels/washcloth
- ☐ deodorant (please!)
- ☐ towelette packets
- ☐ soap
- ☐ toilet paper (two rolls)
- ☐ feminine hygiene items
- ☐ insect repellent/lotion
- ☐ air mattress
- ☐ beach towel
- ☐ shampoo (avoid floral, herbal, or fruit scents)
- ☐ comb/brush
- ☐ items for contact lenses (very difficult to buy there)
- ☐ suntan lotion/sunscreen (very important near the equator)
- ☐ mosquito netting (This is optional; might be good for someone who doesn't like to put on a lot of insect repellent.)
- ☐ personal medicines (Consider vitamins, allergy tabs, caladryl lotion, aspirin, and diarrhea medicine.)
- ☐ travel clothesline
- ☐ servant's attitude
- ☐ notebook for journal/pens
- ☐ flashlight/extra batteries
- ☐ pocket knife
- ☐ Bible
- ☐ passport
- ☐ positive, flexible spirit
- ☐ personal snacks
- ☐ sunglasses
- ☐ spending money (for souvenirs, gifts, occasional meals, etc.)
- ☐ big plastic cup for work site (squeeze bottles work great)
- ☐ cheap watch (maybe to give away when you leave)
- ☐ simple gifts for school children (balloons, balls, etc.)
- ☐ leather work gloves (at least one pair, two would be best)
- ☐ camera/film/batteries (film is generally very expensive overseas)
- ☐ addresses of supporters
- ☐ photos of your family, city, and country (to show new friends and host families)

Clothing

Think about the particular climate when packing.

The following is applicable for work-related teams: T-shirts, cotton socks, bandannas, and underwear are your everyday basics. Work boots (if you are on a construction team), tennis shoes, thongs, hat or sun visor, and a conservative bathing suit are other necessary items.

Men should bring a couple of pairs of work pants, knee-length shorts, and evening-type outfits. Women need to know if they are permitted to work in pants or knee-length shorts. If not, bring loose-fitting, below-the-knee cotton skirts.

Bring comfortable traveling clothes and one or two nice (not extravagant) outfits for church or a nice restaurant.

Luggage: We recommend each person be limited to one large travel/duffel bag and a carry-on with a change of clothes in case luggage is delayed. Since airlines allow two bags and one carry-on per passenger, team members can take an extra suitcase each for work project supplies or other team materials.

Special items: The team leader will instruct you about changes to the packing list as well as additional items not included.

PACKING TIPS

1. *Pack light.* Chances are you will have to carry what you pack!
2. Tightly secure any items that may come open while traveling. Many a team member has had to wear clothing with the fragrant smell of Pepto Bismol or shampoo.
3. Borrow what you can. No sense in making a big investment in shoes and clothing you may only wear on this trip.
4. Break in new shoes before the trip—especially new work boots. Blisters are not a pleasant experience, and they don't make for the best of moods!
5. Take luggage you don't mind damaging. Old duffel bags are probably the best.
6. Carry one change of clothes with you if traveling by plane. Sometimes luggage gets lost and/or delayed. One of the authors failed to heed this advice and lived to regret it when luggage failed to arrive for a two-week trip to Haiti.

---

7. Find out if laundry facilities are available. If so, you won't have to take as much clothing.
8. Take items you won't mind leaving if you see a need. Certain items are very expensive overseas and unaffordable to the people you may be working with.
9. Leave room for souvenirs; otherwise you may be sacrificing your new Reeboks for a wooden statue.
10. Pack more than enough film and batteries. These are costly in most places and may be difficult to find in a remote locale.

BEING A SERVANT

Developing and maintaining a servant's attitude does not come easily or naturally for many of us. Being a servant is something you will understand a great deal better after the trip is over. Each of us needs to encourage one another in servanthood.

Toward Nationals: What does it mean to be a servant to the people of the community and local church? How might this be tested? What attitudes may hinder you from being a servant to the nationals?

Toward the Team Leader: Your team leaders have the same needs and struggles you have. They are doing their best to make the experience a positive and productive one for you. Team leaders really benefit from team members who are willing to seek ways to be a servant to them.

Toward Fellow Team Members: Being a servant toward one another really sums up the whole idea of being a team. Read John 13:1-17 and think through the implications of Jesus washing the disciples' feet. What does that mean for your attitude and relationship with your fellow team members?

For Reflection

Helper or Servant? The dictionary defines to *help* as "to aid, assist or contribute strength; to save or rescue." *Serve* is defined as "to act as the servant of another." What do you see as the difference? What do these definitions say about those who are the object of your help? What do they say about the object of your service?

Wrap-up Discussion Notes
Use this space to record any discussion and comments from your
final meeting together before leaving on the trip.

① used to pack way too much.
Pack too light & will probably
be just right.

② take only ID, Ins Card & Credit
Card if you feel you will
need it.

③ While on the trip & in airports
etc. one person is in charge
Be quiet, stay close, listen
& mind!

④

TRAVEL TIPS

Keep the following in mind while preparing for your trip. Before
you leave, consider where you will be, who you will meet, and
what you will do. Plan ahead.

1. Photocopy your passport and give the copy to the team
   leader for use in case of emergency.
2. Some of the people you meet will enjoy seeing pictures of
   your family and hometown. Be sure to take a few snapshots
   and postcards to show them. (Be sensitive of your audience's
   feelings; your relative affluence may offend some people.)
3. Remember to pack lightly. You will be glad you did!

4. Remember that your dress code will be dictated by the host culture, not your own tastes. Consider leaving all your jewelry behind; this prevents theft as well as the possibility of offending others.
5. Bring small, inexpensive gifts to share with your hosts.
6. Leave your hair dryer at home! Often electrical currents and contact pins are different abroad.
7. Leave a complete itinerary with a friend or family member.
8. Make sure the team leader and your church office have the name, address, and phone number of a contact person for you.
9. Check your wallet and remove anything that won't be needed on the trip. Beware of potential pickpockets while traveling in large cities.
10. Stick with other team members while traveling to avoid being left behind or separated from the group.
11. Write down the flight information if traveling by air in case you do become separated.
12. Upon arrival, hold all your bags tightly while in the crowded and confusing airport.
13. Listen well to the team leader once you arrive at the airport and follow his or her instructions quickly.
14. If traveling by airplane, be aware of the image you are projecting to those around you. Be sensitive to the nationals from your host country who are on board the flight.
15. In many areas, septic systems are not designed to handle toilet paper. If there is a waste receptacle next to the toilet, this is generally a clue that toilet paper is meant to be thrown away, not flushed.
16. If you suffer from any kind of travel sickness, bring proper medication. Remember, it may be difficult for the team to slow down or stop for you to recuperate. Taking these precautions is both helpful and thoughtful.

CHAPTER FIVE

LANGUAGE LEARNING

Foreign language learning. For some, it's an exciting adventure: making strange sounds that somehow have meaning to others, listening for words related to familiar English words, feeling the thrill of understanding someone for the first time. For others, it's a nightmare: incomprehensible sounds coming at a thousand per second, the frustration of not being able to express the most simple sentiment, the mental block that embarrassment produces.

Well, this course is for everyone. The six sessions on the following pages are adapted from a course that has successfully calmed the fears of those nervous around foreign language and encouraged those who love tackling new languages.

A FEW THINGS TO KEEP IN MIND

1. Don't try to learn too much. The information in this chapter is enough without being overwhelming. Work on using proper pronunciation and feel confident with just a few phrases. The late Dr. Tom Brewster of Fuller Seminary encouraged his students to "learn a little, use it a lot!"
2. Don't become frustrated if the language is more difficult for you than for others on the team. There is no need for comparison. The objective is for you to learn what you can!
3. Keep in mind the proper etiquette for speaking English with people who have very little English ability:

   - Speak slowly and clearly.
   - Speaking louder will not help.

- Use common words—if the listener seems confused, think of an alternative word.

4. Be silly and creative. This really should be a fun part of your team preparation!

Goal
Become accustomed to hearing and making new sounds.

◆ **Exercise One**
The alphabet. Letters in other languages are not pronounced the same as they are in English. Learn how each letter is pronounced, including letters that are not in the English alphabet (in Spanish, the letters ch, ll, rr, for example).

◆ **Exercise Two**
Learning names. Write down what your name is in the language.

◆ **Exercise Three**
Song.

SESSION TWO

> **Goal**
> Learn that you probably know more foreign language than you think.

◆ **Exercise One**
Review the alphabet by pronouncing it several times as a group. Then go around the room, one letter at a time.

◆ **Exercise Two**
Introductions. Learn to say, "Hello, my name is _____," using the name you learned last week. Introduce yourself to the other team members.

◆ **Exercise Three**
You will be handed a sheet that has something written in the language you are learning. See if you can figure out what it says.

◆ **Exercise Four**
Vocabulary. Begin learning basic vocabulary related to Scripture and church life.

ENGLISH	SPANISH	OTHER
God	Dios	
Jesus	Jesús	
Jesus Christ	Jesucristo	
the Lord	el Señor	
Protestant	evangélico(a)	
Catholic	Católico(a)	
the Holy Bible	la Santa Biblia	
Matthew	San Mateo	
Mark	San Marcos	
Luke	San Lucas	
John	San Juan	
Acts	Los Hechos	
Praise God!	¡Gloria a Dios!	
we pray	oramos	
to love	amar	

Goal
Begin to build a vocabulary and get a very basic understanding of the grammar.

◆ Exercise One
Review last week's vocabulary.

◆ Exercise Two
Numbers. Learn numbers from one to twenty, plus multiples of ten up to one hundred. Write them below.

NUMBERS			
1 _____		15 _____	
2 _____		16 _____	
3 _____		17 _____	
4 _____		18 _____	
5 _____		19 _____	
6 _____		20 _____	
7 _____		30 _____	
8 _____		40 _____	
9 _____		50 _____	
10 _____		60 _____	
11 _____		70 _____	
12 _____		80 _____	
13 _____		90 _____	
14 _____		100 _____	

◆ Exercise Three
The instructor will teach some *very* basic grammar, not to frustrate and intimidate you, but to help you figure out how words are related to each other.

◆ Exercise Four
Song.

Goal
Be able to introduce yourself to others and give a brief personal description.

◆ **Exercise One**
Review numbers, concentrating on pronunciation.

◆ **Exercise Two**
More vocabulary. Learn the words below to use in saying something about yourself. Write the translation in the blank spaces.

My name is _____.

I have a _____
    Brother _____ Sister _____
    Husband _____ Wife _____
    Child _____ Grandchild _____

I am a _____
    Brother _____ Sister _____
    Husband _____ Wife _____
    Grandfather _____ Grandmother _____

My job is a _____
    Teacher _____ Engineer _____
    Farmer _____ Pastor _____
    Office worker _____ Other _____

The word for my occupation is _____.

I live in the United States _____ Canada _____.

I like _____
    Skiing _____ Animals _____
    Books _____ Sports _____
    Music _____ Other _____

◆ Exercise Three

Ten foods I am likely to encounter.

FOREIGN WORD	SPELLED PHONETICALLY	ENGLISH EQUIVALENT
1.		
2.		
3.		
4.		
5.		
6.		
7.		
8.		
9.		
10.		

◆ Exercise Four

My five-sentence personal description:

◆ Exercise Five

Songs.

Goal
Be able to ask others about themselves.

◆ **Exercise One**
Review all vocabulary to this point, concentrating on last week's.

◆ **Exercise Two**

QUESTIONS FOR CHILDREN
Hello! What's your name?
How old are you?
Do you have brothers and sisters?
What grade are you in?

QUESTIONS FOR ADULTS
Hello! What is your name?
Where do you work?
Where do you live?
What foods do you like?

QUESTIONS FOR PARENTS
How many children do you have?
How old are they?
What is this boy's name?
Does he like school?
What does he like?

◆ **Exercise Three**
Learn another song.

Goal
Instill confidence that you now know at least a few phrases
that can be used in many situations.

◆ Exercise One
Review pronunciation. Look up your favorite verse in a Bible
printed in the foreign language. As you read it aloud, other students should try to guess which verse it is.

◆ Exercise Two
Vocabulary. Learn the survival phrases listed here.

Please.

Thank you.

Please speak more slowly.

One moment, please.

I don't speak much _____.

Do you speak English?

I'm lost. Where is the _____?

I'm sorry

God bless you!

Very good!

I'm tired.

I don't feel well.

Where is the bathroom?

I need a doctor.

◆ Exercise Three
Review all songs.

❖ ❖ ❖

Allelu

Allelu, Allelu, Allelu, Allelujah Alelu, Alelu, Alelu, Alelúia
Praise ye the Lord! **Gloria al Señor!**
Allelu, Allelu, Allelu, Allelujah Alelu, Alelu, Alelu, Alelúia
Praise ye the Lord! **Gloria al Señor!**

Praise ye the Lord! **Gloria al Señor!**
Allelujah! Alelúia!
Praise ye the Lord! **Gloria al Señor!**
Allelujah! Alelúia!
Praise ye the Lord! **Gloria al Señor!**
Allelujah! Alelúia!
Praise ye the Lord! *Gloria al Señor!*

Women stand to sing the first line, then sit. Men stand to sing the second line (bold) then sit. Continue through song, standing each time it's your turn to sing. All stand and sing the final line (italics).

I Love You Lord

I love You Lord Te amo Rey
and I lift my voice, y levanto mi voz,
to worship You. para adorar
Oh my soul rejoice! y gozarme en ti!

Take joy my King Regocíjate,
in what You hear. escucha mi Rey.
Let it be a sweet, Que sea un dulce
sweet sound in Your ear. sonar para ti.

Ho, Ho, Ho, Hosannah

Ho, ho, ho, hosannah Jo, jo, jo, josanah
Ha, ha, hallelujah Ja, ja, jaleluia
He, He, He died for me He, He, El murió por mi
I've got the joy of the Lord! ¡Yo le alabaré!

(Remember, the letter J in Spanish is pronounced like an English H. The H in Spanish is silent.)

PART THREE
GOING

CHAPTER SIX

ON THE FIELD

By now you may be on sensory overload. If this is your first trip abroad, everything may seem to taste, smell, feel, and look different. For some, it may be the first time you've seen a palm tree! For others, this may be your first non-Club-Med vacation. If you've been on a Vacation with a Purpose (VWAP) before, everything may be strangely wonderful and familiar.

Whatever your experience, talk it over with another team member. Get someone else's perspective. Each team member's experience of the first twelve hours in the host country is unique. Responses can be so varied you might even wonder if everyone experienced the same twelve-hour period. Be open to taking in all you can and helping one another process what is happening.

There is no way to anticipate whether you will arrive and be thrust headlong into the people and the project, or have some buffer time before beginning. In either case take a few moments to remind yourself of the reason you are here.

THINGS TO REMEMBER WHILE ON THE TRIP

- *Remember why you are here:* Do you remember the reasons that prompted you to participate on this trip?
- *Remember your financial supporters:* Have you sent them a postcard?
- *Remember your prayer partner(s):* Are you praying for their lives at home just as they are praying for you?
- *Remember your team leader(s):* Are you praying for and encouraging them?

- *Remember the other team members:* Is teamwork and team unity something you have been striving for?
- *Remember the nationals:* Has your interaction with them been marked by a servant's heart?
- *Remember a receptive heart and mind:* Have you been open and listening to how God is speaking to you in the events of each day?

Things do not just "naturally" run smoothly in a Third-World situation. Remembering these suggestions applies the oil of grace to the gears of the trip. Failure to keep them in mind may result in the following disasters, which Rich Hurst humorously outlined.

TEN WAYS TO WRECK A GOOD TRIP

1. Act like you are there alone. Stay to yourself. Isolate others.
2. Think that you are much too important for the work you have been assigned. If dish duty is allocated to you, weasel out of it.
3. Don't pray or study the Bible. You won't have time for it anyway.
4. Be well-organized and inflexible so nothing can interfere with your agenda.
5. Point out what your hosts are doing wrong. Help them improve. Help them be more like you.
6. If you are single, try to become romantically involved with someone on the team. Try to be near that person, even if it means that other team relationships suffer. If you're married, get away frequently to spend time together and to discuss how you'd run things differently if you were the leaders.
7. Don't bother trying to speak the language. Seek out English speakers, then communicate only with them.
8. Point out the faults of people on your team. Try not to be seen with the socially awkward people on the team.
9. Make sure you don't eat the local food. Try to find a grocery store that sells something familiar. If you are forced to eat the local cuisine, complain.
10. Be generally disappointed in how things are going. Whine when things go wrong.

TEAM TIME

Team meetings play an important part in gluing the team together. Times of daily sharing are like an adhesive that mends broken pieces. Do not be afraid to risk your thoughts with the group. You may be the catalyst to a deeper and more meaningful experience for all. This is a place to record significant items discussed or shared in your team meetings. It is also a good place to record your comments from team devotions. This record can jog your memory as to what you and your teammates were learning and going through.

TESTIMONIES/PRESENTATIONS WHILE ON A VWAP

In all likelihood you will be asked to share a brief testimony while on your trip. In our experience, the nationals enjoy hearing about what God is doing in the lives of individual team members. Since many people are unfamiliar with speaking in a different culture, we hope the following tips will be of assistance. Ask your leader to listen to your thoughts before you give the testimony in a church service.

1. Remember, you may have a translator. You may have to pause quite frequently, depending on the skill of the translator. Use simple phrases and avoid slang, which is difficult to translate.
2. Avoid mentioning material possessions you have at home. For example, don't talk about how you learned to trust God when your Porsche was almost stolen!
3. Remember the particular culture. It may be inappropriate to discuss certain topics or activities. (For example, "I met my husband at a church dance.")
4. Keep it brief.
5. Possible subjects to cover are a brief spiritual autobiography or what God has been teaching you while you have been in the country.
6. Communicate your appreciation of the people, the church, the country, the culture.
7. Avoid making negative comparisons between the host culture and your own.
8. Avoid inside jokes between you and your teammates. They only serve to confuse the nationals.
9. Dress properly for the worship service. Customs are not as lax in most other countries when it comes to church attire.
10. Reflect the role of a student instead of a teacher. Avoid large, sweeping suggestions on how they could improve their country.
11. Write down your main points before getting up. This keeps you from going on irrelevant tangents.
12. In addition to hearing testimonies, church members enjoy

   • songs in their language (you've learned a few);
   • hymns and choruses in English, especially sung in harmony;
   • puppet shows and mimes that communicate the message of the gospel; and
   • *anything* else that has been carefully prepared and practiced for their benefit.

Use the space below to record your thoughts as you prepare your testimony. Your notes will be a reminder once you're home of the things you said.

KEEPING TRACK OF MY MONEY

This space is purely for your bookkeeping. Keep track of how much money you have exchanged, and record the exchange rate. Some countries require the exchange of a certain number of American dollars. Your leader will keep you apprised. You may find any number of bargains in the market. Enjoy the bargaining, but don't get so caught up in it that you forget to represent Christ to the vendors.

SOUVENIRS

DONATIONS

MEALS

TOURING

MISCELLANEOUS

CHAPTER SEVEN

MY JOURNAL

The next several pages are for keeping a record of the new things you are seeing, learning, and feeling. Each day's entry includes a suggested Scripture reading, a question for your reflection, a record of the day's events, and a place for you to write your thoughts. The Scripture study and reflection questions are there simply to prompt your journal writing. If you want to write down other things feel free to do so. The better you can identify what you are feeling and learning, the more you will appreciate your journal later.

The journal has entries for a fourteen-day trip. Your trip may be longer or shorter. If it's shorter, you may consider skipping to days thirteen and fourteen for the last two days' entries. If it's longer, consider purchasing a devotional guide.

Try to find time each day to enter something. Remember, your journal should answer the question "What happened in me today?" more than "What happened to me?" When the trip is over, reflect back often and thank God for the things He has shown you.

DAY ONE

Today's Date

Place

What I/we did today:

For Personal Devotion
God knows all about me. (Read Psalm 139.)

For Personal Reflection
Fuller Seminary missions professor Dr. Tom Brewster used to say that no matter what you may think, you *can* learn a language. His advice: "Learn a little, use it a lot." Within one hour of your arrival at the work site, find a non-English speaker and speak to that person using at least one phrase from pre-trip language classes. If possible, enter into a short, basic conversation. Record your impressions from that conversation along with anything else that's on your heart.

Today's Date

Place

What I/we did today:

❖   ❖   ❖

For Personal Devotion
Being like Jesus. (Read Philippians 2:5-11.)

For Personal Reflection
One of the most significant aspects of the gospel is that
Jesus became like us. How can you be like those you serve?
There are numerous answers to that question. For example,
consider the way you dress, the food you eat, the way you
respond to situations, and even the thoughts you think. How
are you using an incarnational approach to cross-cultural
ministry?

DAY THREE

Today's Date

Place

What I/we did today:

❖ ❖ ❖

For Personal Devotion
I became all things to all people. (Read 1 Corinthians
9:19-23.)

For Personal Reflection
Dr. Brewster classifies cross-cultural venturers in three
ways: tourist, adventurer, and explorer. The tourist keeps
his or her distance and observes the new experiences as
an outsider. The adventurer jumps in with both feet and
tries to experience every new thing. The explorer is like the
adventurer but is not satisfied until he or she has broken
new ground. Which are you? Do you approach cross-cultural
travel like you thought you would? (Keep this question in
mind during the rest of the week.)

DAY FOUR

Today's Date

Place

What I/we did today:

For Personal Devotion
Jonah's flight from right. (Read the book of Jonah.)

For Personal Reflection
Get to know one missionary within four days of arrival. Sit down with, or work alongside, the missionary and ask about his or her testimony, decision to become a missionary, life on the mission field, and plans for the future. Record the answers and your impressions here.

Today's Date

Place

What I/we did today:

❖ ❖ ❖

For Personal Devotion
I am your servant. (Read John 13:1-17.)

For Personal Reflection
How are things going in my relationship with my team members? What are the struggles? Why do they exist? Do they have to do with the person, the mission trip, or the bombardment of emotions we feel? What constructive steps am I taking toward resolving the problems? Am I seeing strengths that I never knew existed in one of my friends on the trip? Have I told him or her?

Today's Date

Place

What I/we did today:

❖ ❖ ❖

For Personal Devotion
The first short-term missionaries. (Read Matthew 10:26-32.)

For Personal Reflection
Think about a conversation you have had with someone who
lived in a foreign culture. Or, think about a book you may
have read that deals with a missionary's encounter with a
new culture. Do you recall any of the issues that person dealt
with? Are you confronting those issues now? Consider what
this trip would be like if you were alone and not part of a
group. What if this were the first week of several years in
this culture?

DAY SEVEN

Today's Date

Place

What I/we did today:

For Personal Devotion
We're all parts of one Body. (Read 1 Corinthians 12:12-31.)

For Personal Reflection
Which spiritual gifts are emerging or being reinforced in me as a result of my participation on this team?

DAY EIGHT

Today's Date

Place

What I/we did today:

For Personal Devotion
Part of the team. (Read 1 Corinthians 3:5-11.)

For Personal Reflection
How do you feel knowing that you are just a part of God's larger plan? Does it make you feel insignificant? Why is your part important?

DAY NINE

Today's Date

Place

What I/we did today:

❖   ❖   ❖

For Personal Devotion
God cares for the oppressed. (Read Psalm 10.)

For Personal Reflection
Have you seen oppression here? Does God seem to stand far
off, or does He see the trouble and the grief?

DAY TEN

Today's Date

Place

What I/we did today:

◆ ◆ ◆

For Personal Devotion
Too busy with "service"? (Read Luke 10:38-42.)

For Personal Reflection
Is it possible to be too busy doing "the Lord's work" to have time for God? Are you doing that now on this trip? Do you do so at home?

DAY ELEVEN

Today's Date

Place

What I/we did today:

❖　❖　❖

For Personal Devotion
Giving your all. (Read Luke 21:1-4.)

For Personal Reflection
In what ways have you seen people giving to God their "last two copper coins"?

DAY TWELVE

Today's Date

Place

What I/we did today:

❖ ❖ ❖

For Personal Devotion
The wicked and the pure. (Read Psalm 73.)

For Personal Reflection
Do you get angry that the "wicked" prosper, while the "pure" suffer? Do you feel confused? Have you learned anything on this trip that helps you grapple with this difficult issue?

DAY THIRTEEN

Today's Date

Place

What I/we did today:

For Personal Devotion
How will they know, if no one shows them? (Read Acts 8:26-40.)

For Personal Reflection
During the past several days you have probably thought about ways to continue your involvement with Third-World Christians, or with the poor at home. You may want to tell others about God's power to work in the world and in people's lives. Resolve now to take at least one substantive step toward blending this past week's experiences with your future commitments and convictions.

DAY FOURTEEN

Today's Date

Place

What I/we did today:

❖ ❖ ❖

For Personal Devotion
Bless the Lord, O my soul! (Read Psalm 103.)

For Personal Reflection
Tomorrow you will be home. During the past days you have been confronted by a variety of new sights, tastes, ideas, etc. Make a list below of the moments, the experiences, and the revelations that you want to be sure never to forget.

CHAPTER EIGHT

THE GOOD-BYS

Are you wondering how you will be able to say good-by to your new friends? Are you prepared for that emotionally draining experience? You are leaving friends you have grown to love and may never see again. You are bringing closure to a profound time of growth. And you may find that both you and your hosts shed tears as you take your leave.

Throughout the Vacation with a Purpose (VWAP) you may have looked forward to returning home to the friends, family, car, ice, and flush toilets that await you. But on the last day these desires seem curiously distant and unimportant. Leaving tears at your heart. It puts a hole in your heart that only your new friends can fill. We need to remember that these good-bys are not forever. Believers have eternity to be together. And then language will be no barrier! This ending is really only a prologue to a greater adventure that awaits those who love the Lord.

The following items may help you keep your good-bys in perspective, even if they seem to make them no easier.

1. *Do not be afraid to show and express emotion.* More than likely the nationals have fewer inhibitions than you, so learn from them! Hugs and words of appreciation are expressions you will not regret.
2. *Treasure the moment.* So often we live our lives for the future and fail to appreciate the present moment. This is a good moment, one that cannot be duplicated. So be present and value what is happening.

3. *Get the addresses of those you intend on writing.* Do not make commitments to everyone. Be realistic. That will help you have integrity at home and abroad.
4. *Give a small gift as a token of your friendship.* The giving of gifts should not be elaborate because that may introduce awkwardness into the friendship. Rather, choose something personal that will remind the person of you.
5. *Talk about your feelings with the team after you have departed.* This will create an environment where others may feel it's okay to share their grief and joy.
6. *Do not expect others to handle the good-bys as you do.* We all respond differently to emotionally charged events. Be accepting of others' inhibitions or tears.
7. *Get plenty of photographs or video footage.* You (and perhaps only you) will value this once at home. You may also want to send photographs to the host community once you're home. (Be sure photographs and video are appropriate in the host community.)
8. *Agree to pray for one another.* This is the most important expression of love you may be able to share with your newfound friends. Let them know they will be in your prayers.
9. *Avoid making financial commitments during the good-by phase.* You may confuse a very valuable time by introducing finances into your farewells. Furthermore, you might make a commitment you are unable to keep once home. Wait and think through your financial decisions.

ADDRESS SHEET FOR NEW FRIENDS

Use this space to record addresses and other information (e.g., birthdays) of people whom you meet in the country/region.

CHAPTER NINE

DEBRIEFING

Can you believe it's nearly time to begin traveling home? Back to "regular" life . . . whatever that is!

It is a mistake to think you can jump easily from one world into the next or from this experience into the nine-to-five routine. You need an adjustment period. Allow yourself to have it.

You may feel uneasy or self-conscious or even guilty about taking some R & R after living amid need and want. But this time is necessary for integrating your experience in the host community with your experience of plenty at home. We live in a world of many heartbreaking contrasts. And it is important to know what God would intend our responses to be.

People will have different reactions and learn different things from their VWAP. Do not judge others on the basis of what God is doing in you. Your call to be faithful may not be like somebody else's. But pay attention to what God is teaching you. Take the extra hours you have during the R & R to reflect, pray, and make some decisions about your life back home. Is there another team member you can meet with on a regular basis for prayer? Does someone need to hold you accountable for choices you are going to make?

The R & R portion is not meant solely for reflection; it is also for recreation. So enjoy. God rejoices in our fun as well as our work when we do it unto Him.

The following material may help you think through the reality of entering life back at home. Be sure to talk through these tips with others on your team.

TIPS FOR ENTERING LIFE BACK HOME

Don't expect too much from other people. People may be too busy to listen to you as much as you expect them to. They won't be as excited about your trip as you are (not even your close family and friends). Remember, they had their own experiences while you were gone. Keeping your expectations low allows you to be pleasantly surprised by those who show great interest.

Share briefly. People do not want to hear everything that happened to you. Stifle the tendency to take them through a day-by-day account. They'll lose interest about midway through the second day!

Be careful about value judgments. Do not argue with people about values. It is counterproductive and alienates them. Upon your return, you may tend to be judgmental about the values in American culture. We all need to reevaluate our lifestyles from time to time, but it's not up to us to determine others' convictions for them. The Holy Spirit is far more effective than a censorious spirit. Let them see a changed life.

Do not be critical of others' spirituality. God may be teaching others in ways you do not understand. Just because you went on this trip and learned what you did does not give you the right to be critical of others.

Be prepared for nostalgia. Sometimes you may long to be back in the country. You may ache to be back with some of the nationals that became your friends. And believe it or not, you may even want to be back with some of your teammates! Expect those feelings and be prepared for them.

Don't let a little depression take you by surprise. When feelings of nostalgia hit, you may experience a little depression. Others go through it too, so call a teammate and talk with him or her about what you are feeling. Remember, you are not alone!

Be cautious about negative reporting. Things may have happened on your trip that were not to your liking. They are fresh in your mind now, but time will give you perspective on them. If you are very critical and negative in your reporting, you do a disservice to others and the VWAP. Share the tough experiences in light of what God taught you and the team through them.

Try to stay in touch with one or two individuals you met on your trip. Receiving a letter may help you remember the good experiences you had.

Contact your prayer partners and financial supporters. Of all the people back home, these will be the most interested in your trip. We suggest you make this contact as personal as your situation allows. Thank them for their prayers and support. Ask them to pray for you as you readjust to daily living.

Develop some realistic, practical applications for yourself. Avoid making unreasonable demands on yourself like, "I am going to pray for every missionary in that country for an hour every day." Think through some realistic ways of integrating your experiences into your daily routine at home.

PART FOUR
GETTING HOME

CHAPTER TEN

BACK-AT-HOME STUDY MATERIAL

The following material is meant to help you think through the entire Vacation with a Purpose (VWAP) experience. You may tend to procrastinate because things are *so* busy once you are home. However, to maximize what you have experienced on your trip, you should take time during your first month home to work through this material. We also suggest discussing this material with at least one other team member.

The trip that was the focus of so much energy, time, and money is over. Went by quickly, didn't it? Does it seem like only yesterday that you were looking through the "what to bring" list and frantically running out to the discount store to get all the little necessities? Remember wondering how in the world you would ever get everything packed in just two suitcases? You needed a miracle on the scale of the parting of the Red Sea!

If you are like others who have gone, you are probably experiencing a wide range of emotions and thoughts at this time. There's a sense of loneliness now that you are not with your team members twenty-four hours a day (and perhaps a sense of thankfulness too!). It felt good to have friends around who were experiencing many of the same things. There was always some-one to share and pray and laugh with. There's a sense of having touched something very real and significant. And there is the question of what it all means to your everyday life. You may feel the need to do something with your experience. But what form ought it to take? Lastly, there can be an enormous amount of exhaustion creating a desire, at least for the moment, to file away this "missions stuff" or "world need stuff."

Now, while things are still fresh in your mind, is the time to process your experience. Think through what you saw while in the country and with the people. Reflect on the situations in which you lived and served. Go back and try to relive the feelings you had when you were confronted with needs. How did you feel about yourself and your life? Thinking through the trip will help you focus on the main issue you face at home: What will be your response now that you are back?

A VWAP experience is a special gift. Yes, you had a hand in making it happen. But more than likely, a number of things came together to make your participation possible. Wasn't God the One who orchestrated your going? Why did He choose you? Is this unique "vacation" simply another experience to be filed away in your memory banks? Chances are high that if you take time to reflect on and analyze your trip you will find much that could radically impact your lifestyle and choices. But that's a big if. Some come back and figure they'll think about it "one of these days." All too quickly they get caught up in the pace and stress of daily living. They're too busy to draw all they could out of the trip. Ignore, for the moment, a few of the daily demands on your time and draw away and allow God to guide you in understanding the implications of your trip. Do it now.

The following four sections will help you in that process. Please do them in the order given and avoid the tendency to rush. Keep in mind that you are doing this for yourself—no one else. Make an appointment with yourself to do each section in the next two weeks.

The euphoria will eventually evaporate. The daily routine gradually disperses it. But it's not the euphoric feelings that are going to matter six months or a year from now. What matters are the memories, and the lessons, and the choices that were precipitated by your VWAP.

WHAT I SAW

Begin by remembering the different things you saw on the trip—both the expected and the unexpected.

One thing is for sure: your eyes were *open* while you were there. Does that sound like a ridiculous statement? How could one's eyes not be open? Yet very often in our everyday lives we go through our routines and never "see" things. We are too busy or too preoccupied to notice them. But it was different on your trip; you had prepared yourself to "see." You were determined to observe the various things you would encounter each day. Take some time now to reflect upon what you saw.

The People

1. What did you see in the people that you did not expect to see?

2. Which of their needs are most vivid in your memory?

3. What aspects of their lives impressed you most?

The Country

4. What things did you see in the country that were different from your expectations?

5. Is there any picture that quickly comes to mind? (Briefly describe it and the reasons it has stayed with you.)

Seeing is a discipline we develop. It is the first step in making a difference in our world. Unless one sees the needs, one can never meet the needs.

Because you were willing to keep your eyes open on the trip you probably "saw" quite a bit. Not merely sights and sounds all jumbled together, but needs, issues, and concerns festering beneath the surface. We hope that what you saw will stick with you and, more importantly, you will continue to keep your eyes open.

Jesus admonished the disciples to "open their eyes and see," an admonition well suited for His disciples today as well. So many Christians live without ever seeing. Perhaps you were one of them before this trip. Now the question is not only whether you will remember what you saw in the countries you were in, but whether you will continue to "see" each and every day.

6. What keeps you from "seeing" your world?

WHAT I LEARNED

As your experience in and knowledge of the host country has grown, perhaps some ignorance in your perspective about the world and its inhabitants has been dispelled. We hope you took time to listen and learn from those you encountered. Take time to reflect upon what you have learned.

7. List two things you learned about each of the following:

a. The people

b. The country

c. The church in the country

d. The people on your team

e. Yourself

8. Which of the above surprised you? Why?

9. Look back over the "needs" you noted "seeing" (question 2) and rephrase them here.

Needs do not simply appear out of nowhere. Rather, there are factors that contribute to their existence. If we understand these factors, we are better able to identify with the people and to work with them in meeting their needs.

10. What factors have contributed to the needs of the people you were with? (Think through the sociological, political, spiritual, emotional, and physical factors you may have heard about.)

Understanding our world requires effort. Far too often, people put forth no effort to become educated to the situations around them. Seeing needs is a necessary beginning, but without understanding what we see we can be of little help. The question for you to consider is, now that you have seen and understood the people's needs, will your life be the same as it had been before you went on the trip?

11. What keeps people from learning about and understanding the needs in their world?

WHAT I FELT

The writers of the gospels tell us that whenever Jesus Christ encountered people in need He was deeply moved by what He saw. He felt the pain of their need and situation. During your time in the country there were probably situations that caused you to feel deeply. As you saw a particular person or an incident, you may have been "deeply moved." In those times you were most likely being challenged by God in some way.

12. a. Think of at least one situation on your trip when you really "felt deeply" about something. Write a description of the situation.

   b. What was it you "felt"? (Try to describe the feelings you had at that moment.)

c. Were you surprised by your feelings? Why?

13. As you reflect back on that situation, what growth do you think God had in mind for you in those feelings?

Feelings come and go, there's no doubt about that. Yet, the feelings you experienced on this trip may be etched in your memory forever. And their memory may prompt you to feel deeply again and again in the world in which you live. God meant for you to go on this trip. And He will continue to challenge you to grow. Will you pay Him the same sort of attention now as you did on your trip? He is not through with you yet.

14. What factors may prevent you from being "deeply moved" in the world in which you live?

HOW WILL I RESPOND?

Now comes the tough but exciting part: the application of what you saw, learned, and felt. What are you going to do with your experience? How are you going to respond to the things God is teaching you?

It is one thing to go on a trip and have a great time. Many do. But it is quite another to go on a trip and allow the experience to change you and the world in which you live. The process of responding is an ongoing one that requires you to make decisions day by day. It requires ongoing action. Your trip only began a process. The process is not finished. In this section, instead of reflecting on the trip, think about the present.

15. a. What changes have you made in your life as a result of what you have seen, learned, and felt on this trip?

    b. Why those changes?

16. Think in terms of three areas of possible ongoing responses to the world you live in.

    a. How might you use your time differently based on what you have experienced?

    b. How might you use your money or resources differently based on what you have experienced?

c. How might you adjust your lifestyle based on what you have experienced?

17. What ideas do you have for remembering the people you met and the experiences you had?

WAYS TO STAY INVOLVED ONCE YOU RETURN

The previous questions will help you think about your response in general terms. Now, think about specific responses. The following are just a few ways former VWAP participants have integrated the experience into their lives.

Mission committee membership and/or participation in the church's mission conference. One team member had never considered being involved in any of his church's mission activities. After his VWAP, he became active on committees and educated himself about the concerns in areas where his church's missionaries were working. He also began contributing more of his monthly income to missions.

Further language study. One woman, after a trip to the Dominican Republic, investigated language classes at a local junior college. She decided to enroll and study Spanish in the hopes of being able to communicate more effectively the next time she traveled in Spanish-speaking areas.

Involvement with international students through local universities or ministries to international students. This is a great opportunity to return the hospitality shown you by your host community. Many international students want to experience North American homes and ways of life.

Monthly support of a child through a child sponsorship agency. Nancy began sponsoring a child at an orphanage in Mexico. The relationship grew to be more than merely a financial one, however. In the ensuing years she made several trips to the orphanage to spend time with the child. In addition, visitors to Nancy's apartment quickly notice the numerous photographs and letters from her special little girl.

Further study of the religious, economic, social, and political situations related to the host culture. This is often done by former participants who, as North American Christians, want to increase their understanding of the host culture so they can respond appropriately to important issues.

Involvement in local community ministries. Holly participated on a team that worked at a school for the deaf. As a direct result of her experience, she changed her major in college to deaf communications and is currently working as a liaison between the state government and the local deaf community.

Writing notes of encouragement and praying for missionaries and host community members. Many VWAP participants who hardly concerned themselves with the lives and work of missionaries or people of other cultures prior to their trip, became very active in the support of missionaries and nationals through their money, prayer, and correspondence.

Involvement in longer-term, cross-cultural missionary service. One team member joined a VWAP team to investigate her sense of being called by God to serve overseas. She took one day off from the work site to interview with a mission agency operating in the city where she was interested in utilizing her gifts as a teacher. Six months later, she was back in the country as a missionary.

CHAPTER ELEVEN

COMMUNICATING THE EXPERIENCE

Going on a VWAP is a little like pulling up to a gas station and filling your tank with premium fuel. You feel supercharged about your experiences. But if you aren't careful, you can run people down in your enthusiasm to tell *all* that happened to you. Your experience can fuel others, but you need to remember that some people already have full tanks while others' are on empty. Ask God to give you sensitivity in explaining your experience to others. He can prepare hearts to hear, just as He can prepare you to speak.

Your financial supporters and prayer partners will be the most interested group. Remember, they invested in it. It is a mistake to neglect them once you are home.

Very often we run to tell our friends about the trip and show them the pictures, but we neglect to run to our supporters. Then we wonder why they're not all that interested in becoming involved again in a VWAP in the future. Keep in mind that your experience is partially owned by them. You were the one who was able to go, but they had a part in making the whole thing happen.

Communicating to these people is also a great opportunity for you to broaden their interest in world need. You may well be their closest contact to the global community. By sharing your experience, people of different cultures/countries become more than just images on a TV screen. Do not underestimate this potential.

The following are suggestions that others have used. Use these as a springboard for your own creative ideas.

1. *Send a letter to all supporters.* Include at least one photo of the people, the work, the church, or some significant event. Personalize these as much as possible to avoid the appearance of a form letter.
2. *Bring back little gifts for your supporters.* These do not need to be elaborate, but simply something from the culture. Everyone enjoys and appreciates getting a small token of appreciation.
3. *Have a dinner party and invite supporters to view your slides/photographs/video.* Some people have even attempted to cook a national dish and serve it.
4. *Share with them not only what you did and learned but what you intend to do with the experience.* Communicate the applications you intend to attempt to make to your life.
5. *Communicate to them how they might become involved.* Gently and sensitively share challenges with them. (If they are financial supporters, be cautious about asking for money again so soon.)

CHURCH PRESENTATIONS

Chances are, you and your team will be asked to give a presentation at your church. (If you are not asked, make the offer to the appropriate people.) Your leader(s) will be helpful here, but in case you are on your own, the following ideas will be of help. Remember, the more effectively you communicate about your trip, the more likely others will want to be involved in the future.

1. *Use slides when possible.* Visual aids help communicate what you saw and experienced. However, be careful not to overdo it. Some may be delighted you took 500 pictures, but their delight does not translate into a desire to see all 500! Show only as many as necessary to communicate your trip. As a trial run, show your slides to a non-team member prior to a big presentation. One group puts the slides to music and produces an interesting and moving multimedia presentation. Since they use several projectors, they can use more slides and still keep the whole presentation moving along quickly.

2. *Keep it short and to the point.* People do not want a day-by-day, feeling-by-feeling, meal-by-meal account of the trip. They were not there and cannot possibly comprehend every aspect of your experience. Boring them will be a turnoff to the whole VWAP idea.
3. *Focus on how your life is different because of what you have seen and experienced.* People find that to be both interesting and challenging.
4. *Communicate appreciation for being able to go.* Do not come across as arrogant or self-righteous. These people more than likely provided you the opportunity.
5. *Do not preach.* As anyone in the church knows, we have enough fine preachers. What we often need are peers who share their lives and insights with us.

Common Mistakes
The list below includes the most common complaints teams have heard from the audiences about their presentations:

- The team put too many expectations on the presentation.
- It was too long!
- There were too many slides, or too much *unedited* video.
- It was too team-oriented. The team wasn't thinking about their audience.
- The team was too demanding. They wanted everyone to have some sort of response to their message (trying to play Holy Spirit).
- There was too much criticism of our own culture.
- They were too critical of Christianity at home.
- There was too much talk and too little action.

CHAPTER TWELVE

NOW WHAT?

Remember reading, "When God wants to teach you something, He takes you on a trip"? Part one of your trip is completed. But you are still on a pilgrimage. And God will continue to reap fruit from the seeds that were planted during your VWAP. We encourage you to let this book be a reminder and a marker of God's work in your life.

The content of this book is not so much written material as it is faces of people, moments with God, laughs and tears shared with old and new friends, and stretching times with self. This book is a kind of written photo album. And we encourage you to leaf through its pages as years go by.

The freshness of the memories will fade with time, but glancing through this book can revive them and rekindle in you the call to live out the responses you once felt challenged to make. All of us need to dust off the memories from time to time in order to remember things that became so important to us on this trip.

Now what? We hope you are on the path to becoming more of a world Christian in your daily living. Unless we live this out in our daily lives, our VWAP runs the risk of becoming only another tour or some benevolent endeavor. For many of you, the process of thinking as a world Christian began the first day you filled out your application. Now it will continue beyond this book and beyond this VWAP, if you choose to let it. The choice is yours. What will it be?

RECOMMENDED READING LIST

Borthwick, Paul. *A Mind for Missions*. Colorado Springs, CO: NavPress, 1987.

Campolo, Anthony. *Who Switched the Price Tags?* Waco, TX: Word Books, 1986.

Engel, James F., and Jerry D. Jones. *Baby Boomers and the Future of World Missions*. Management Development Associates, 1989.

Hawthorne, Steven, and Ralph D. Winter, eds. *Perspectives on the World Christian Movement*. Pasadena, CA: William Carey Library, 1981.

Johnstone, Patrick. *Operation World*. Pasadena, CA: STL Books, 1986.

Kane, Herbert J. *Wanted: World Christians*. Grand Rapids, MI: Baker Book House, 1986.

Lappe, Frances Moore. *World Hunger: Twelve Myths*. New York: Grove Press, 1986.

Larson, Bruce. *Faith for the Journey*. Old Tappan, NJ: Fleming H. Revell Co., 1982, 1986.

Nash, Ronald H. *Liberation Theology*. Grand Rapids, MI: Baker Book House, 1988.

Sider, Ron. *Rich Christians in an Age of Hunger.* Downers Grove, IL: InterVarsity Press, 1977.

Sine, Tom. *The Mustard Seed Conspiracy.* Waco, TX: Word Books, 1981.

Sine, Tom. *Why Settle for More and Miss the Best?* Waco, TX: Word Books, 1987.

Stepping Out: A Guide to Short-Term Missions. Short-Term Missions Advocates, Inc., 1987 (P.O. Box 6018, Evanston, IL 60204).

Tremblay, Helene. *Families of the World: Family Life at the Close of the 20th Century (The Americas & The Caribbean).* New York: Farrar, Straus and Giroux, 1988.

Warner, David, trans. *Where There Is No Doctor.* Palo Alto, CA: Hisperian Foundation, 1977.